A Note From Rick Renner

I am on a personal quest to see a "revival of the Bible" so people can establish their lives on a firm foundation that will stand strong and endure the test when the end-time storm winds begin to intensify.

In order to experience a revival of the Bible in your personal life, it is important to take time each day to read, receive, and apply its truths to your life. James tells us that if we will continue in the perfect law of liberty — refusing to be forgetful hearers but determined to be doers — we will be blessed in our ways. As you watch or listen to the programs in this series and work through this corresponding study guide, I trust that you will search the Scriptures and allow the Holy Spirit to help you hear something new from God's Word that applies specifically to your life. I encourage you to be a doer of the Word that He reveals to you. Whatever the cost, I assure you — it will be worth it.

> Thy words were found, and I did eat them;
> and thy word was unto me the joy and rejoicing of mine heart:
> for I am called by thy name, O Lord God of hosts.
> — Jeremiah 15:16

Your brother and friend in Jesus Christ,

Rick Renner

The Love Test

Copyright © 2020 by Rick Renner

8316 E. 73rd St.

Tulsa, Oklahoma 74133

Published by Rick Renner Ministries

www.renner.org

ISBN 13: 978-1-68031-808-1

eBook ISBN 13: 978-1-68031-809-8

How To Use This Study Guide

This five-lesson study guide corresponds to *"The Love Test" With Rick Renner* (Renner TV). Each lesson in this study guide covers a topic that is addressed during the program series, with questions and references supplied to draw you deeper into your own private study of the Scriptures on this subject.

To derive the most benefit from this study guide, consider the following:

First, watch or listen to the program prior to working through the corresponding lesson in this guide. (Programs can also be viewed at **renner.org** by clicking on the Media/Archives links.)

Second, take the time to look up the scriptures included in each lesson. Prayerfully consider their application to your own life.

Third, use a journal or notebook to make note of your answers to each lesson's Study Questions and Practical Application challenges.

Fourth, invest specific time in prayer and in the Word of God to consult with the Holy Spirit. Write down the scriptures or insights He reveals to you.

Finally, take action! Whatever the Lord tells you to do according to His Word, do it.

For added insights on this subject, it is recommended that you obtain the Renner Short Reads *The Love Test* by Rick Renner and *The Gift of Forgiveness* by Denise Renner. You may also select from Rick's other available resources by placing your order at **renner.org** or by calling 1-800-742-5593.

TOPIC

Do You Sound Like a Sounding Brass or a Tinkling Cymbal?

SCRIPTURES

1. **1 Corinthians 13:1** — Though I speak with the tongues of men and of angels, and have not charity, I am become as sounding brass, or a tinkling cymbal.

GREEK WORDS

1. "brass" — χαλκός (*chalkos*): metal; bronze or copper to which a small amount of tin had been added; the tin caused the metal to have a hollow, empty sound when it was beaten

2. "sounding" — ἠχέω (*echeo*): a noise that reverberates or echoes; used to depict the nonstop roaring of the sea

3. "sounding brass" — the endless beating of metal that produces a hollow, annoying, irritating echo that seems to eternally reverberate

4. "tinkling" — ἀλαλάζον (*alalazon*): to clash or to crash loudly; there is nothing 'tinkling' about it

5. "cymbal" — κύμβαλον (*kumbalon*): cymbal

6. "tinkling cymbal" — used together, describes a constant, loud clashing of cymbals, much like the clashing cymbals played by the Jewish people just before they went to war; the clashing of those cymbals was a call to arms; it sounded the signal that it was time to fight

SYNOPSIS

The five lessons in this study on *The Love Test* will focus on the following topics:

- Do You Sound Like a Sounding Brass or a Tinkling Cymbal?
- Love Is Patient, Kind, and Not Self-Focused

- Love Vaunts Not Itself, Is Not Puffed Up, and Does Not Behave Itself Unseemly
- Love Seeks Not Its Own, Is Not Easily Provoked, Thinks No Evil
- Love Never Fails

The emphasis of this lesson:

Through the apostle Paul, God instructs us to walk in love with one another. Without love, we come across like 'sounding brass or a tinkling cymbal.' That is, we are an annoying, irritating sound that seems to eternally echo in people's ears. The love of God visibly at work in and through our lives is what gets people's attention and draws people to Him.

God Has Called Us To Walk in Love

Located in downtown Moscow is a bridge that is situated on a waterway right between the Kremlin and the Tretyakov Gallery. It is called the Bridge of Love, and it is very important to Muscovites. When many of the local couples get married, they come to this bridge on their wedding day to fasten a special, personalized lock onto one of the seven trees nearby. By doing so, they are saying to everyone, "We're in love, and we're locked to each other for the rest of our lives."

This visual expression of love may be the easiest thing they do to demonstrate their commitment. Actually walking in love on a day-to-day basis will be the most challenging thing they do in life. Indeed, real love calls for a life of sacrifice. As a matter of fact, for any relationship to be at its best, we have to be willing to become each other's servant. That is what God calls us to do as Christians — to walk in love with each other.

In First Corinthians 13, the apostle Paul gives us what many have called *The Love Test*. This passage of Scripture has been read at countless weddings and preached about in numerous messages. Paul opens the chapter saying, "Though I speak with the tongues of men and of angels, and have not charity, I am become as sounding brass, or a tinkling cymbal" (1 Corinthians 13:1). The word "charity" in this verse and throughout this chapter is the Greek word *agape*, which describes the purest kind of love there is — the God-kind of love, which is totally unconditional and selfless. So when you see the word "charity," it means love.

Paul went on to write in First Corinthians 13:4-8:

> Charity [love] suffereth long, and is kind; charity [love] envieth not; charity [love] vaunteth not itself, is not puffed up, doth not behave itself unseemly, seeketh not her own, is not easily provoked, thinketh no evil; rejoiceth not in iniquity, but rejoiceth in the truth; beareth all things, believeth all things, hopeth all things, endureth all things. Charity [love] never faileth....

Wow! These verses are so powerful. What is interesting about them is that not only do they describe the love God has for us, they also describe the kind of love He wants us to have for one another. As we walk through this series, we will take a close look at the original Greek meanings of the key words in this passage and see just how well we score at walking in love. For now, let's begin by examining the meaning of our anchor verse — First Corinthians 13:1.

Paul Painted a Picture the Corinthian Believers Understood

In order to better understand what Paul is saying in First Corinthians 13:1, it is helpful to understand the background of this verse. Apparently, Paul had encountered a group of people in the city of Corinth who were projecting themselves as being deeply spiritual. These Corinthians said they spoke in the tongues of men and even in the tongues of angels. Although they presented themselves as being super spiritual, Paul knew otherwise. Their actions didn't match their spiritual claims. To put it plainly, there was no demonstration of love in their lives, and to be around these people was absolutely sickening.

Have you ever met anyone like this? You know — someone who claims to have profound revelations from God and is constantly boasting about all the amazing things they are doing. This is the type of person that when you see them coming, you want to run in the opposite direction as fast as you can. Even if he or she does have profound revelations from God, the fact that they are so self-absorbed and lack the love of God in their life is just nauseating. These are the kind of people Paul had encountered while in Corinth that prompted him to write First Corinthians 13:1: "Though I speak with the tongues of men and of angels, and have not charity, I am become as sounding brass, or a tinkling cymbal."

When Paul said, "…and have not charity [love]," the word "have" is a form of the Greek word *echo*, which means *to have, to hold*, or *to possess*. In the context here, Paul was saying, "If I speak with the tongues of men and angels but do not *have* or *hold* or *possess* love in my life, I have become as sounding brass or a tinkling cymbal."

What Is 'Sounding Brass'?

The word "brass" in First Corinthians 13:1 is the Greek word *chalkos*, which describes *metal*, and in this case it indicates *bronze or copper to which a small amount of tin had been added*. The added tin caused the metal to have a hollow, empty sound when it was beaten.

Now this "brass" is not ordinary. It's "sounding" brass. The word "sounding" is a translation of the word *echeo*, which describes *a noise that reverberates or echoes and it seems it will never stop*. This word was also used to depict *the nonstop roaring of the sea*. If you have ever been near the sea during a storm, you understand how deafening the sound can be and how the noise is impossible to escape.

When Paul coupled these two words together — "sounding brass" — he was describing *the endless beating of metal that produces a hollow, annoying, irritating echo that seems to eternally reverberate*. What you may not know is that he borrowed this imagery from a common activity in the pagan environment in Corinth, as well as in the pagan cities of Ephesus, Rome, Athens, Pergamum, Laodicea, and every other major city that was filled with paganism.

In the pagan world there were religious fanatics, and these fanatics wanted to attract spiritual entities to them. They believed that if they would perpetually bang their musical instruments — which were made of brass, bronze, or copper — and would just keep banging on them endlessly, the false entities they worshiped would come to them.

Pagan priests used the perpetual banging and clanging to not only attract more demonic entities, but also to drive the pagan people into a frenzied state of ecstasy. Under the influence of drugs and wine, pagan worshipers would dance wildly as the pagan priests banged harder and faster on their instruments. It seemed impossible to escape their never-ending nuisance of noise.

The Corinthian believers to whom Paul was writing clearly understood what he was describing. Corinth was a very spiritually dark place filled with pagan temples and activities. Thus, the phrase "sounding brass" is the picture of pagan worshipers, frantically and endlessly banging on their musical instruments. The sound they produced echoed throughout the city and was extremely annoying.

This phrase "sounding brass" eventually came to denote people who talk incessantly and are just like the non-stop clanging of the pagan worshipers. They are so consumed with themselves and their own revelations and self-importance that they never shut up. Paul said these individuals are a shallow, empty, irritating clanging noise to those around them.

What Is a 'Tinkling Cymbal'?

Paul went on to add that these same people are like a "tinkling cymbal" (*see* 1 Corinthians 13:1). When you hear the word "tinkling," you may think of a small insignificant sound, but it is actually just the opposite. In Greek, the word "tinkling" is *alalazon*, which means *to clash or to crash loudly; there is nothing 'tinkling' about it*. It is *a non-stop crashing and clashing* of a "cymbal," which is the Greek word *kumbalon*, describing a *cymbal*.

When these two words are joined to form the phrase "tinkling cymbal," it describes *a constant, loud clashing of cymbals, much like the clashing cymbals played by the Jewish people just before they went to war.* The clashing of those cymbals was a call to arms; it sounded the signal that it was time to fight. Hence, "sounding brass and a tinkling cymbal" was something nerve-racking and irritating. It aroused one's emotions, making him or her fighting mad.

These are the words the Holy Spirit prompted Paul to use to describe a person who claims to be spiritually great but doesn't demonstrate love in his life. This individual can become such an irritant to you that you will want to go to war with them. They are so self-absorbed and self-focused that they never ask about you or anyone else.

Taking into account the original Greek meaning of these words, here is the *Renner Interpretive Version (RIV)* of First Corinthians 13:1:

> **Even if I converse fluently in the languages of men and of angels, but do not possess love, then it's all nothing more than empty, hollow sounds. People like this, who claim to**

be super-spiritual but lack love, sound a lot like the nonstop banging and clanging of pagan brass instruments in your city that you wish would stop. Those who go around pretending to be deeply spiritual, but who are sorely deficient in love, are so annoying that when you feel trapped in a vicinity near them, you'll begin to look for any way to escape from being trapped with them. Even if they may say all the right things, their lack of love makes them as grating on your nerves as the clanging brass instruments that make you want to scream, 'Stop it and stop it now!' Let's be honest — these super-spiritual motor-mouths talk incessantly about how spiritual they are, but their absence of love makes it nothing more than a bunch of verbal hullabaloo. The hyped-up spiritual talk of these folks who demonstrate zero love to match their words is so offensive and nauseating that it can nearly call your flesh to battle just to get them to shut up.

Note: the *RIV* is the *Renner Interpretive Version* of a particular verse or passage. Moreover, it is an interpretive and conceptual translation of the New Testament that draws on pictorial concepts in the Greek language and interprets them in a contemporary way to provide a broader comprehension of what is being communicated through Scripture.

Instead of Exploding in Anger, Put Yourself in Their Shoes

With these kinds of people, you need extra grace from God to be patient and deal with them in love. Although they may truly have revelations from God, it is extremely hard to receive what they have to say because of the pride that seems to ooze from them. Instead of slapping them or tearing into them verbally, what they really need is for you to confront them by speaking the truth *in love*. The best thing you can do for someone like this is to pray for the opportunity for you — or someone else — to speak the truth in love to them.

What if *you* were the person people were repelled by and wanted to avoid? What if it was *your* words and actions that were pushing people away? If the tables were turned and you were the one who was like "sounding brass and a tinkling cymbal," wouldn't you want someone to be patient with *you* and speak the truth in love?

One thing is certain: We will always have these kinds of irritating people with us. Therefore, we need the Spirit of God to do a work in us to be able to love them and deal with them like Jesus Himself would. We need to have His heart, His mind, His words, and His timing to say what these people need to hear. But before we say anything to anyone, we need to make sure everything is right within our own heart.

In our next lesson, we will continue to explore First Corinthians 13 and see what else the Holy Spirit spoke through the apostle Paul about walking in love.

STUDY QUESTIONS

Study to shew thyself approved unto God, a workman that needeth not to be ashamed, rightly dividing the word of truth.
— 2 Timothy 2:15

1. Who is the "motor-mouth" in your life that is driving you crazy with their spiritual self-importance? It is the person you cringe at seeing and seek to avoid if at all possible.

2. Instead of slapping them silly or tearing into them verbally, how does God want you to respond to them? (*Consider* Ephesians 4:15 and 25, and Zechariah 8:16.)

3. If the tables were turned and *you* were the one who was like "sounding brass or a tinkling cymbal," how would you want someone to respond to *you*? What would be the best attitude with which they could approach you? What words do you think would be best for them to speak to really get through to you?

PRACTICAL APPLICATION

But be ye doers of the word, and not hearers only,
deceiving your own selves.
— James 1:22

1. Have you ever been around a person who was like "sounding brass"? They talked and talked about themselves incessantly and you couldn't wait to get away from them? What was it specifically about their actions that irritated and frustrated you most?

2. When you encounter a person who brags of being spiritually superior but is severely lacking in love, how do you normally respond?

3. Sometimes the things we see in others that we don't like are the very things we ourselves are doing (*see* Romans 2:1). Pause for a moment and pray, *"Lord, is there something You are trying to show me about myself from this person in my life who is like "sounding brass"? Is there something selfish and unloving in my character that I've been blind to that You are trying to show me so that it can be removed? If so, what is it?"*

TOPIC

Love Is Patient, Kind, and Not Self-Focused

SCRIPTURES

1. **1 Corinthians 13:1** — Though I speak with the tongues of men and of angels, and have not charity, I am become as sounding brass, or a tinkling cymbal.

2. **1 Corinthians 13:4-8** — Charity suffereth long, and is kind; charity envieth not; charity vaunteth not itself, is not puffed up, doth not behave itself unseemly, seeketh not her own, is not easily provoked, thinketh no evil; rejoiceth not in iniquity, but rejoiceth in the truth; beareth all things, believeth all things, hopeth all things, endureth all things. Charity never faileth....

3. **Romans 5:5** — And hope maketh not ashamed; because the love of God is shed abroad in our hearts by the Holy Ghost which is given unto us.

GREEK WORDS

1. "charity"— ἀγάπη (*agape*): a divine love that gives and gives, even if it's never responded to, thanked, or acknowledged; this love occurs when an individual sees, recognizes, understands, or appreciates the value of an object or a person, causing the viewer to behold this object or person in great esteem, awe, admiration, wonder, and sincere appre-

ciation; such great respect is awakened in the heart of the observer for the object or person he is beholding that he is compelled to love it; a love for a person or object that is irresistible; a love so profound that it knows no limits or boundaries in how far, wide, high, and deep it will go to show that love to its recipient; a self-sacrificial love that moves the lover to action

2. "suffereth long" — μακροθυμία (*makrothumia*): compound of the words μακρός (*makros*) and θυμός (*thumos*); the word μακρός (*makros*) means long and may indicate something that is long or of long duration; the word θυμός (*thumos*); means anger, but also embodies the idea of swelling emotions or a strong and growing passion about something; compounded, it forms the word *makrothumia*, which pictures the patient restraint of anger and therefore longsuffering; forbearance and patience; it doesn't easily give up or bow out

3. "shed abroad" — ἐκχέω (*ekcheo*): a pouring forth, discharge, spilling out, or something dispersed in abundance; liberally and lavishly poured out

4. "kind" — χρηστεύομαι (*chrestos*): portrays helpfulness, warmheartedness, and a willingness to show goodness from the heart to others — a trait so admirable in the ancient world that it was viewed as a characteristic that everyone should seek to possess; pictures one who is attentive to the needs of others, who is beneficial and helpful to others, or who is considerate of other people and their needs and demonstrates this kindness in some way; depicted those in positions of authority who were kind, mild, and benevolent to their subjects; anyone who demonstrated this quality was considered to be compassionate, considerate, sympathetic, humane, kind, and gentle; when applied to interhuman relationships, it conveys the idea of being adaptable to others; to be adaptable or compliant to the needs of others

SYNOPSIS

Moscow is a magnificent city in many ways, and it was to this city that God called Rick and Denise Renner and their family nearly 30 years ago. Situated in the central part of town is a bridge called the Bridge of Love, and it is very special to Muscovites. Countless brides and grooms have made the journey to this bridge on their wedding day to attach a special lock onto one of the seven huge trees that line the way. It is their way of declaring their love for one another for the rest of their lives.

Although putting a personalized lock on one of these trees can easily be done, learning to walk in love will be a different matter altogether. True love requires great surrender and a life of self-denial. For a marriage to truly flourish, the husband and wife must choose to lay down their lives for one another, just as Jesus laid His life down for the Church. That is what God calls us to do as Christians — to walk in love with each other.

The emphasis of this lesson:

God's love for you is unparalleled! It has been abundantly poured into your heart by the Holy Spirit the moment you were saved. Unlike human, natural love, God's *agape* love is unconditional, sacrificial, and totally selfless. It is supernaturally longsuffering and kind to others, displaying great patience and adaptability.

If you have ever looked for a passage of Scripture that tells you how to live your life as a Christian, First Corinthians 13 would definitely be one of them. Here, the apostle Paul gives us a mirror we are to look into to see if we are reflecting the love of God. Paul begins the chapter saying, "Though I speak with the tongues of men and of angels, and have not charity [love], I am become as sounding brass, or a tinkling cymbal" (1 Corinthians 13:1). As we noted in the first lesson, the word "charity" in this verse and throughout this chapter is the Greek word *agape*, which describes the purest kind of love there is — the *God-kind of love*, which is totally *selfless* and *unconditional*. When you see the word "charity," it signifies God's *agape love*.

Paul went on to write:

> **Charity [love] suffereth long, and is kind; charity [love] envieth not; charity [love] vaunteth not itself, is not puffed up, doth not behave itself unseemly, seeketh not her own, is not easily provoked, thinketh no evil; rejoiceth not in iniquity, but rejoiceth in the truth; beareth all things, believeth all things, hopeth all things, endureth all things. Charity [love] never faileth....**
> **1 Corinthians 13:4-8**

These five verses paint a picture of true love — God's *agape* love — and how it acts. In this lesson, we will focus on the meaning of the first part of verse 4: "Charity [love] suffereth long, and is kind...." But first, let's review how love does *not* behave in First Corinthians 13:1.

A Review of Our Anchor Verse

As we saw in our first lesson, Paul had encountered a group of people in Corinth who were projecting themselves as deeply spiritual, but they had no demonstration of love in their lives. This experience prompted him to write, "Though I speak with the tongues of men and of angels, and have not charity [love], I am become as sounding brass, or a tinkling cymbal" (1 Corinthians 13:1).

Paul said these *big talkers* were people who claimed to be super spiritual but didn't "have" love in their lives. The word "have" is a form of the Greek word *echo*, which means *to have, to hold,* or *to possess.* Hence, these people who boasted of their great spiritual revelations did not *have* or *hold* or *possess* love in their actions. Consequently, they were the equivalent of "sounding brass, or a tinkling cymbal."

The phrase "sounding brass" described *the endless clanging and banging of metal instruments* that pagan priests played in the streets to attract spiritual entities and drive pagan worshipers into a frenzied state. This non-stop beating of metal produced a hollow, annoying, irritating echo that caused people to cover their ears and do whatever they could to escape the sound. Eventually, the words "sounding brass" came to denote people who talk incessantly about themselves and are consumed with their own revelations but void of God's love.

This brings us to the phrase "tinkling cymbal," which is *alalazon kumbalon* in Greek, and it describes *a constant, loud clashing of cymbals, much like the clashing cymbals played by the Jewish people just before they went to war.* The clashing of those cymbals was a call to arms; it sounded the signal that it was time to fight. Thus, "sounding brass and a tinkling cymbal" was something nerve-racking and extremely irritating.

In the context of First Corinthians 13:1, Paul said, "Those who claim to be super spiritual — speaking in the tongues of men and angels — but lack the love of God operating in their lives are just an annoying, irritating, hollow noise that drives people crazy."

Taking into account the original Greek meaning of these words, here is the *Renner Interpretive Version (RIV)* of First Corinthians 13:1:

> **Even if I converse fluently in the languages of men and of angels, but do not possess love, then it's all nothing more**

than empty, hollow sounds. People like this, who claim to be super-spiritual but lack love, sound a lot like the nonstop banging and clanging of pagan brass instruments in your city that you wish would stop. Those who go around pretending to be deeply spiritual, but who are sorely deficient in love, are so annoying that when you feel trapped in a vicinity near them, you'll begin to look for any way to escape from being trapped with them. Even if they may say all the right things, their lack of love makes them as grating on your nerves as the clanging brass instruments that make you want to scream, 'Stop it and stop it now!' Let's be honest — these super-spiritual motor-mouths talk incessantly about how spiritual they are, but their absence of love makes it nothing more than a bunch of verbal hullabaloo. The hyped-up spiritual talk of these folks who demonstrate zero love to match their words is so offensive and nauseating that it can nearly call your flesh to battle just to get them to shut up.

God's *Agape* Love Is Incomparable!

When we come to First Corinthians 13:4, Paul begins to describe the true nature of God's love by saying, "Charity [love] suffereth long, and is kind...." In Greek, the word "charity" is a translation of the word *agape*, which is the primary word for "love" in the New Testament. The word *agape* describes *a divine love that gives and gives, even if it's never responded to, thanked, or acknowledged*. This lets us know that God's *agape* love has no strings attached to it, and it can never be offended.

God's *agape* love occurs when an individual sees, recognizes, understands, or appreciates the value of an object or a person. It causes the viewer to behold this object or person in great esteem, awe, admiration, wonder, and sincere appreciation. *Agape* love awakens such great respect in the heart of the observer for the object or person he is beholding that he is compelled to love it.

Furthermore, *agape* love is *love for a person or object that is irresistible; a love so profound that it knows no limits or boundaries in how far, wide, high, and deep it will go to show that love to its recipient*. It is *a self-sacrificial love that moves the lover to action*. Clearly, God's *agape* love is magnificent and unlike anything we could generate in our own strength.

The word *agape* describes *the highest level of love that exists in the world,* and it is the level of love that God wants every believer to walk in. It is a love so completely different from what the world offers that it is the word always used to describe the love of God. Indeed, it is a divine, supernatural kind of love that is both unconditional and sacrificial. Have you received God's unconditional, agape love, and are you walking in it?

God's Love 'Suffereth Long'

The first description Paul gives us for the agape love of God is that it "...suffereth long..." (1 Corinthians 13:4). The phrase "suffereth long" is the Greek word *makrothumia*, a compound of the words *makros* and *thumos*. The word *makros* means *long* and may indicate *something that is long or of long duration.* The word *thumos* means *anger*, but it also embodies *the idea of swelling emotions* or *a strong and growing passion about something.* When these two words are compounded to form the word *makrothumia*, it pictures *the patient restraint of anger and therefore longsuffering.* It can also describe *forbearance* and *patience.* Thus, "suffereth long" or "long suffering" describes *something that doesn't easily give up or bow out.*

A good, practical example of the word "suffereth long" — the Greek word *makrothumia* — is a candle that has a very long wick. Think about it: a candle with a long wick is equipped to burn a very long time. You might say it is ready to *forbear* and *patiently wait* until a person finally comes around and sees the light. Or, someone is *forbearing* and *patient* with a person until that person finally grasps what is being communicated or taught to them.

Using this illustration, a person who "suffereth long" does not easily give up or bow out. Instead, he keeps steadily burning and burning and burning. Spiritually speaking, he has a very long wick and has made the decision to hang in there and not give up — even though the other person is unresponsive and shows no signs of change.

Taking into account the original Greek meaning of this word, here is the *Renner Interpretive Version (RIV)* of this part of First Corinthians 13:4:

> **Love patiently and passionately bears with others for as long as patience is needed and does not easily give up or bow out.**

Unlike frail, human love, which eventually says, "I'm sick and tired of waiting for this person to change. That's it — I'm out of here," God's *agape* love never throws in the towel. The longer the struggle, the more committed *agape* love is for that person. It is totally supernatural!

God's Love Is 'Kind'

In addition to being long suffering, First Corinthians 13:4 says God's agape love is also "kind." The word "kind" is a translation of the Greek word *chrestos*, which portrays *helpfulness, warm-heartedness, and a willingness to show goodness from the heart to others* — a trait so admirable in the ancient world that it was viewed as a characteristic that everyone should seek to possess. This word *chrestos* pictures *one who is attentive to the needs of others, who is beneficial and helpful to others, or who is considerate of other people and their needs and demonstrates this kindness in some way.*

Moreover, this word depicted *those in positions of authority who were kind, mild, and benevolent to their subjects.* Anyone who demonstrated this quality was considered to be compassionate, considerate, sympathetic, humane, kind, and gentle. When applied to inter-human relationships, this attribute of being "kind" conveys the idea of *being adaptable to others; to be adaptable or compliant to the needs of others.*

That's how love operates — it is "kind" — *chrestos.* When God's high-level, *agape* love is operating in your life, you want to be a blessing to others. Instead of demanding that others change to be like you, you become *adaptable to others* and *compliant to their needs.* Rather than get frustrated and say, "If you don't like it, you can lump it," *agape* love in you goes the extra mile, becoming what others need to help meet their needs.

Taking into account the original Greek meaning of these words, here is the *Renner Interpretive Version (RIV)* of this part of First Corinthians 13:4:

> **Love doesn't demand others to be like itself; rather, it is so focused on the needs of others that it bends over backwards to become what others need it to be.**

God's *agape* love is the exact opposite of selfishness, which insists on its own rights and its own ways. When God's love is operating in your life, you are focused on others and compelled to love them. In fact, you are so compelled to love them that you are longsuffering with them — willing to keep the light of hope burning and burning until they finally respond or come around and change.

God's Love Is *in You*

Now, you may be thinking, *Wow! God's love certainly is amazing, but I just don't know if I have it in me to love on that level.* But the truth is, you do. The Bible says, "…The love of God is shed abroad in our hearts by the Holy Ghost which is given unto us" (Romans 5:5). According to this verse, the agape love of God has been shed abroad in the heart of every believer — including yours.

In Greek, the phrase "shed abroad" describes *a pouring forth, a spilling out,* or *something that is dispersed in abundance.* In other words, the moment you surrendered your life to Jesus and made Him your Lord and Savior, God liberally and lavishly poured His *agape* love into you. So, since you have it in you, the key is learning how to release it in your life. This comes by humbling yourself and asking the Holy Spirit to help you walk in love daily.

Friend, if you are wise, it is in your best interest to look into the mirror of First Corinthians 13 and see if you are walking in the high-level, *agape* love that God wants you to walk in. If you see areas where you are coming up short, ask Him for strength to make the needed adjustments in your life.

STUDY QUESTIONS

Study to shew thyself approved unto God, a workman that needeth not to be ashamed, rightly dividing the word of truth.
— 2 Timothy 2:15

It is vital for you to realize that love is not just something God does — it is who He is. First John 4:8 declares, "…God is love." Friend, God loves you — yes *you* — more than words can say. The question is: do you have a revelation of His love? Look up these verses and personalize God's amazing promises to you about His love. (The first one is done for you as an example.)

- **Romans 5:8** – God demonstrated His love for *me* in this: while *I* was still a sinner, Christ died for *me.*
- **John 3:16,17** – _____

_____

- **Romans 8:35-39** – _____

- **Ephesians 2:4,5** – _____

- **1 John 3:1** – _____

PRACTICAL APPLICATION

But be ye doers of the word, and not hearers only,
deceiving your own selves.
—James 1:22

1. Do you know — *really know* — that God loves you? Have you accepted and received His love? If not, why? What is hindering you from receiving His love?

2. Friend, there is nothing you have done or could do that can keep God from loving you! If you have confessed your sins to Him and repented, according to First John 1:9, He has forgiven you and cleansed you from all unrighteousness. If you're struggling to believe God loves you, pray: *"Holy Spirit, please help me to know that I know that God loves me. Give me a deeper revelation of His love for me. In Jesus' Name, Amen."*

3. Romans 5:5 says, "…The love of God is shed abroad in our hearts by the Holy Ghost which is given unto us." Are you experiencing God's *agape* love flowing through you? If not, take time now to pray. Say, *"Holy Spirit, please help me. I want to walk in God's love, but I'm struggling. Please unlock the agape love that has been deposited within me and enable me to be longsuffering and kind just like Jesus. In His name I pray. Amen."*

TOPIC
Love Vaunts Not Itself, Is Not Puffed Up, and Does Not Behave Itself Unseemly

SCRIPTURES

1. **1 Corinthians 13:1** — Though I speak with the tongues of men and of angels, and have not charity, I am become as sounding brass, or a tinkling cymbal.

2. **1 Corinthians 13:4,5** — Charity suffereth long, and is kind; charity envieth not; charity vaunteth not itself, is not puffed up, doth not behave itself unseemly....

GREEK WORDS

1. "suffereth long" — **μακροθυμία** (*makrothumia*): compound of the words **μακρός** (*makros*) and **θυμός** (*thumos*); the word **μακρός** (*makros*) means long and may indicate something that is long or of long duration; the word **θυμός** (*thumos*); means anger, but also embodies the idea of swelling emotions or a strong and growing passion about something; compounded, it forms the word *makrothumia*, which pictures the patient restraint of anger and therefore longsuffering; forbearance and patience; it doesn't easily give up or bow out

2. "kind" — **χρηστεύομαι** (*chrestos*): portrays helpfulness, warm-heartedness, and a willingness to show goodness from the heart to others — a trait so admirable in the ancient world that it was viewed as a characteristic that everyone should seek to possess; pictures one who is attentive to the needs of others, who is beneficial and helpful to others, or who is considerate of other people and their needs and demonstrates this kindness in some way; depicted those in positions of authority who were kind, mild, and benevolent to their subjects; anyone who demonstrated this quality was considered to be compassionate, considerate, sympathetic, humane, kind, and gentle; when applied to interhuman relationships, it conveys the idea of being

adaptable to others; to be adaptable or compliant to the needs of others

3. "envy" — ζηλόω (*zelos*): depicts one who is self-consumed and who is driven to see his agenda adopted; one who is competitive; pictures one who is upset because someone else achieved more or received more; one who is jealous, envious, resentful, and filled with ill will for that one who got what he wanted; irritated, infuriated, irate, annoyed, provoked, and fuming; one who is incensed; portrays one who is radically consumed with his own desires and plans

4. "vaunteth" — περπερεύομα (*perpereuomai*): a lot of self-talk; pictures one who endlessly promotes himself and exaggerates his own virtues; this self-promotion is so outrageous that is usually prone to exaggeration that borders on lying; one Greek scholar notes that the word *perpereuomai* pictures a person who is full of hot air; another expositor has said this word refers to a windbag

5. "puffed up" — φυσιόω (*phusio*): proud, swollen, or inflated; portrays one who is filled with pride; one who has an air of superiority and haughtiness; one who is snooty or snobbish in his dealings with other people; a self-inflated individual; a clannish feeling by a group who believes they are superior to others

6. "unseemly" — ἀσχημονέω (*aschemoneo*): to act in an unbecoming manner; a person who is tactless or thoughtless; a person who is careless and inconsiderate of others; one whose actions and words tend to be rude and discourteous; one who exhibits bad manners in the way he deals with people; one whose language is harsh, brutal, uncaring, insensitive, and unkind; one who acts ugly

SYNOPSIS

As we have noted in the previous lessons, there is a very special bridge in downtown Moscow, which has come to be known as the Bridge of Love. On one side of it sits the Kremlin, and on the other side is the Tretyakov Gallery. The reason this bridge has grown to be cherished by many Muscovites in recent years is because of the sentimental symbolism attached to it. Countless local couples have made their way to this landmark on their wedding day to attach a personalized lock to one of the seven trees that line the road. It is their way of saying to each other and the world, "*We're committed to walking in love for the rest of our lives.*"

Attaching a symbolic lock to a tree is much easier than actually walking in love with others on a daily basis. Think about it. Walking in love with your spouse, your children, people at church, and people at work can be extremely difficult at times. But through the power of the Holy Spirit and the love of God that has been deposited in our hearts, we can obediently walk in love with one another.

The emphasis of this lesson:

When God's love is working in our lives, we are not envious, self-promoting, proud, rude, or ill-mannered. We become others-centered instead of self-centered; we are humble and speak truthfully about ourselves. God's love in us is respectful and courteous of others, being considerate and mindful of their needs.

A Review of Our Anchor Verse
1 Corinthians 13:1

First Corinthians 13 is known by many as The Love Chapter, and in this passage, we find *The Love Test*. In these verses, the apostle Paul gives us a mirror to gaze into to see if our lives are truly reflecting the love of God and where we need His strength to come up higher. In verse 1 of our anchor verse, Paul said, "Though I speak with the tongues of men and of angels, and have not charity, I become as sounding brass, or a tinkling cymbal." As we noted in the first lesson, the word "charity" in this verse and throughout this chapter is the Greek word *agape*, and it describes the purest kind of love there is — the *supernatural love of God*. Therefore, when you see the word "charity," know that it means God's *agape* love.

As we saw in Lessons 1 and 2, Paul had come across a group of believers in Corinth who were putting on airs of being deeply spiritual, but they were not demonstrating the love of God in their lives. Paul likened these individuals to "sounding brass, or a tinkling cymbal" (1 Corinthians 13:1).

The phrase "sounding brass" described *the endless clanging and banging of metal instruments* that pagan priests played in the streets to attract spiritual entities and drive pagan worshipers into a frenzied state. Eventually, the words "sounding brass" came to denote people who talk incessantly about themselves and are consumed with their own revelations but are void of God's love.

The words "tinkling cymbal" describe *a constant, loud clashing of cymbals, much like the clashing cymbals played by the Jewish people just before they went to war.* Thus, "sounding brass and a tinkling cymbal" was something nerve-racking, annoying, and extremely irritating. Essentially, Paul said, "Those who claim to be super spiritual — speaking in the tongues of men and angels — but lack the love of God operating in their lives are just an annoying, irritating, hollow noise that drives people crazy."

Taking into account the original Greek meaning of these words, here is the *Renner Interpretive Version (RIV)* of First Corinthians 13:1:

> **Even if I converse fluently in the languages of men and of angels, but do not possess love, then it's all nothing more than empty, hollow sounds. People like this, who claim to be super-spiritual but lack love, sound a lot like the nonstop banging and clanging of pagan brass instruments in your city that you wish would stop. Those who go around pretending to be deeply spiritual, but who are sorely deficient in love, are so annoying that when you feel trapped in a vicinity near them, you'll begin to look for any way to escape from being trapped with them. Even if they may say all the right things, their lack of love makes them as grating on your nerves as the clanging brass instruments that make you want to scream, 'Stop it and stop it now!' Let's be honest — these super-spiritual motor-mouths talk incessantly about how spiritual they are, but their absence of love makes it nothing more than a bunch of verbal hullabaloo. The hyped-up spiritual talk of these folks who demonstrate zero love to match their words is so offensive and nauseating that it can nearly call your flesh to battle just to get them to shut up.**

God's *Agape* Love
'Suffereth Long and Is Kind'

In Lesson 2, we examined the first half of First Corinthians 13:4 in which Paul wrote, "Charity [love] suffereth long, and is kind...." We saw that the phrase "suffereth long" in Greek is the word *makrothumia*, a compound of the words *makros* and *thumos*. The word *makros* describes *something long* or *something that is of long duration*; the word *thumos* carries *the idea of swelling emotions* or *a strong and growing passion about something*. When these two words are compounded to form the word *makrothumia*, it pictures *the patient restraint of anger and therefore longsuffering.* It can also describe *forbearance* and *patience.* Thus, a person who "suffereth long" is *one that doesn't easily give up or bow out.*

This tells us that when love is manifesting through your life in the form of *longsuffering,* you are like a candle with a long wick that is equipped to burn for a very long time. You are ready to *forbear* and *patiently wait* until the person you're working with or believing for finally comes around and changes — or finally grasps what you are trying to communicate or teach them.

Taking into account the original Greek meaning of these words, here is the *Renner Interpretive Version (RIV)* of the first part of First Corinthians 13:4:

Love patiently and passionately bears with others for as long as patience is needed and does not easily give up or bow out.

So longsuffering — the Greek word *makrothumia* — is evidence of the genuine agape love of God operating in one's life. It does not throw in the towel and quit. In fact, the longer and more intense the struggle, the more committed it is to suffer long and forebear. There is nothing natural about this; it is the supernatural love of God.

In addition to being longsuffering, Paul said the love of God is also "kind." We saw that the word "kind" is a form of the Greek word *chrestos*, which portrays *helpfulness, warm-heartedness, and a willingness to show goodness from the heart to others.* It is a trait so admirable in the ancient world that it was viewed as a characteristic that everyone should aspire to have. The word *chrestos* pictures *one who is attentive to the needs of others, who is beneficial and helpful to others, or who is considerate of other people and their needs and demonstrates this kindness in some way.*

Furthermore, this word depicted *those in positions of authority who were kind, mild, and benevolent to their subjects.* Anyone who demonstrated this quality was considered to be compassionate, considerate, sympathetic, humane, kind, and gentle. When we apply this attribute to inter-human relationships, being "kind" — the Greek word *chrestos* — conveys the idea of *being adaptable to others, or compliant to the needs of others.*

This lets you know that when God's *agape* love is operating in you, you are "kind." This means instead of demanding that others change to be like you, you become *adaptable to others* and *compliant to their needs*. Rather than get frustrated and say, "If you don't like it, you can lump it," *agape* love in you is willing to bend over backwards to be whatever you need to be to reach others and help meet their needs. Thus, real *agape* love is not selfish or self-focused; it is focused on others.

Taking into account the original Greek meaning of this word, here is the *Renner Interpretive Version (RIV)* of this part of First Corinthians 13:4:

> **Love doesn't demand others to be like itself; rather, it is so focused on the needs of others that it bends over backwards to become what others need it to be.**

GOD'S *AGAPE* LOVE…
'Envieth Not'

In the second part of First Corinthians 13:4, Paul went on to say that love "…envieth not…." The Greek word for "envy" here is the word *zelos*, and it depicts *one who is self-consumed and who is driven to see his agenda adopted; one who is competitive*. This word pictures *one who is upset because someone else achieved more or received more; one who is jealous, envious, resentful, and filled with ill will for that one who got what he wanted*. The word *zelos* — translated here as "envieth" — also denotes *one who is irritated, infuriated, irate, annoyed, provoked, and fuming*, or *one who is incensed*. Furthermore, it portrays *one who is radically consumed with his own desires and plans*.

A person who is envious is one who is bent on getting his own way. In fact, he is so fixated on what he wants that he is willing to sacrifice anything, or anyone, to get what he wants. This person is the epitome of selfish ambition and self-centeredness. He is so self-focused that he never thinks about those around him or the needs that they have. Therefore, a person who is operating in the *agape* love of God is the exact opposite of one who is envious.

Taking into account the original Greek meaning of this word, here is the *Renner Interpretive Version (RIV)* of this part of First Corinthians 13:4:

Love is not ambitious, self-centered, or so consumed with itself that it never thinks of the needs or desires that others possess.

'Vaunteth Not Itself'

As we continue to read First Corinthians 13:4, we see from Paul's description that love also "…vaunteth not itself.…" At first reading, the words "vaunteth not itself" seem very strange. This is an old King James phrase that we don't use today. It is actually a translation of the Greek word *perpereuomai*, which describes *a lot of self-talk*. It is *a picture of one who endlessly promotes himself and exaggerates his own virtues.* This self-promotion is so outrageous that it is usually prone to exaggeration that borders on lying. One Greek scholar notes that the word *perpereuomai* pictures *a person who is full of hot air*, and another expositor has said this word refers to *a windbag.*

Taking into account the original Greek meaning of this word, here is the *Renner Interpretive Version (RIV)* of this part of First Corinthians 13:4:

> **Love doesn't go around talking about itself all the time, constantly exaggerating and embellishing the facts to make it look more important in the sight of others.**

'Is Not Puffed Up'

Besides not being envious or self-promoting, the Bibles says that love "…is not puffed up" (1 Corinthians 13:4). This phrase "puffed up" is the Greek word *phusio*, which means *to be proud, swollen, or inflated*. It portrays *one who is filled with pride; one who has an air of superiority and haughtiness;* or *one who is snooty or snobbish in his dealings with other people.* It depicts *a self-inflated individual.* Moreover, the word *phusio* — translated here as "puffed up" — can also describe *a clannish feeling by a group who believes they are superior to others.*

Taking into account the original Greek meaning of this word, here is the *Renner Interpretive Version (RIV)* of this part of First Corinthians 13:4:

> **Love does not behave in a prideful, arrogant, haughty, superior, snooty, snobbish, or clannish manner.**

'Doth Not Behave Itself Unseemly'

When we come to First Corinthians 13:5, Paul continues his description of love, telling us that God's love, "doth not behave itself unseemly...." Here again, we see wording that is awkward and unfamiliar. The word "unseemly" in this verse is the Greek word *aschemoneo*, which means *to act in an unbecoming manner*. It is the picture of *a person who is tactless or thoughtless; one who is careless and inconsiderate of others*. This person's actions and words tend to be *rude and discourteous*. He or she exhibits bad manners in the way he or she deals with people. It is *one whose language is harsh, brutal, uncaring, insensitive, and unkind*. The bottom line: a person who is "unseemly" is *one who acts ugly*. Thus, when the genuine *agape* love of God is working in you, you are not tactless, thoughtless, or ugly with others.

Taking into account the original Greek meaning of this word, here is the *Renner Interpretive Version (RIV)* of this part of First Corinthians 13:5:

> **Love is not rude and discourteous — it is not careless or thoughtless, nor does it carry on in a fashion that would be considered insensitive to others.**

When we include the original Greek meaning of all the words we've studied so far, here is the *Renner Interpretive Version (RIV)* of First Corinthians 13:4 and the first part of verse 5:

> **Love patiently and passionately bears with others for as long as patience is needed and does not easily give up or bow out; love doesn't demand others to be like itself, but is so focused on the needs of others that it bends over backwards to become what others need it to be; love is not ambitious, self-centered, or so consumed with itself that it never thinks of the needs or desires that others possess; love doesn't go around talking about itself all the time, constantly exaggerating and embellishing the facts to make it look more important in the sight of others; love does not behave in a prideful, arrogant, haughty, superior, snooty, snobbish, or clannish manner; love is not rude and discourteous — it is not careless or thoughtless, nor does it carry on in a fashion that would be considered insensitive to others**

Chances are, you are probably thinking of at least one person that fits the description of being envious, self-promoting, puffed up, and/or unseemly.

This is a person who makes you want to run in the opposite direction as soon as you see him or her. He or she is so self-absorbed, self-centered, and self-focused that this person never asks one question about you or anyone else. Although this person claims to be super-spiritual, his or her actions are void of God's *agape* love. As a result, this person is perceived as offensive and even disgusting.

Friend, this is exactly the opposite of what we want to be. Rather than be preoccupied with ourselves, God wants us to be rooted and grounded in His love. When God's agape love is working in us and flowing through us to others, we become so secure and confident that we don't need to talk about ourselves or our accomplishments. We are free to focus on others — bringing them encouragement, hope, strength, and meeting their needs. That is what agape love does — it gives.

In our next lesson, we will continue our journey through First Corinthians 13 and see what the Bible means when it says that love *seeks not its own, is not easily provoked*, and *thinks no evil.*

STUDY QUESTIONS

Study to shew thyself approved unto God, a workman that needeth not to be ashamed, rightly dividing the word of truth.
— 2 Timothy 2:15

1. It has often been said that we can't give to others what we ourselves don't have. In other words, you can't give others the *agape* love of God until you have first received it yourself. Carefully read Paul's prayer for the believers in Ephesians 3:14-19 (in the Amplified Bible if possible). Knowing that this passage was written under the direction of the Holy Spirit, what does God want to happen in *your* life?

2. According to James 4:6, First Peter 5:5, and Proverbs 3:34, why is *pride* in your life so detrimental? Why is pursuing *humility* so important? What other blessings come with humility? (*See* Proverbs 11:2; 22:4; 29:23.)

3. Take a moment to reflect on the *Renner Interpretive Version (RIV)* of First Corinthians 13:4 and the first part of verse 5 at the end of this lesson. Are you passing *The Love Test?* In what areas do you feel you are walking in God's love? Where do you need His help to come up

higher? What is the Holy Spirit speaking to you personally through this contemporary interpretation?

PRACTICAL APPLICATION

**But be ye doers of the word, and not hearers only,
deceiving your own selves.
—James 1:22**

1. As we went through this lesson, did a certain person's name or an image of their face flash on the screen of your mind who shows God's love? If so, who is it? Would you say their actions are *giving* and *focused on others*? What lessons can you learn from their example and incorporate in your own life?

2. One of the facets of God's love is that He is *longsuffering* — He is ready to *forbear* and *patiently wait* until you finally come around and see the light — finally grasping what He is trying to communicate or teach you. Looking back on your life, in what area or areas can you see where God has been *longsuffering* with you? How does your gratefulness for His enduring patience motivate you to be longsuffering to others?

3. What practical steps might you take to begin demonstrating God's love more and more in every area of your life?

TOPIC

Love Seeks Not Its Own, Is Not Easily Provoked, Thinks No Evil

SCRIPTURES

1. **1 Corinthians 13:1** — Though I speak with the tongues of men and of angels, and have not charity, I am become as sounding brass, or a tinkling cymbal.

2. **1 Corinthians 13:4,5** — Charity suffereth long, and is kind; charity envieth not; charity vaunteth not itself, is not puffed up, doth not behave itself unseemly, seeketh not her own, is not easily provoked, thinketh no evil.

3. **Acts 15:39,40** — And the contention was so sharp between them, that they departed asunder one from the other and so Barnabas took Mark, and sailed unto Cyprus; and Paul chose Silas, and departed....

4. **Psalm 103:12** — As far as the east is from the west, so far hath he removed our transgressions from us.

GREEK WORDS

1. "seeketh" — ζητέω (*zeteo*): in a negative sense, depicts one so upset about not getting what he wants that he turned to the court system to sue or to demand what he wanted to obtain; a person so intent on getting his own way that he will search, seek, and investigate, never giving up in his pursuit to get what he wants; it could denote a scheming individual who manipulates people, events or circumstances to get what he wants

2. "provoked" — παροξύνω (*paroxsuno*): a compound of παρά (*para*) and ὀξύς (*oxsus*); the word παρά (*para*) means alongside; the word ὀξύς (*oxsus*) means to poke, to prick, or to stick, as with a sharpened instrument; compounded, portrays someone who comes alongside another and then begins to poke, prick, or stick that other person with some type of sharpened instrument; he continues to poke, prick,

and stick until the victim becomes provoked; to call into combat; to irritate, to incite, to anger, to inflame, or to enrage; to provoke

3. "thinketh" — λογίζομαι (*logidzomai*): to mathematically count, calculate, or tabulate or to make a conclusion; to keep records; used in the bookkeeping world to portray the idea of a balance sheet or a profit-and-loss statement that a bookkeeper prepared at the end of the month or year; to make a calculation

SYNOPSIS

Moscow, Russia, has been the hometown of Rick and Denise Renner and their sons for many years. From this historic city, their ministry reaches out across the globe with the Good News of Jesus! Not too far from their offices are the Kremlin Palace, the Tretyakov Gallery, and a massive statue of Peter the Great. Amidst these famous landmarks is what Muscovites call the Bridge of Love. Traditionally, couples travel to this location on their wedding day. They make a declaration of their love by attaching a lock with their names on it to one of the seven large trees that line the bridge.

As exciting as wedding ceremonies of this nature may be, love can be very fleeting without making a true commitment to walk in the highest level of love there is. What we are talking about is the *agape* love of God, which is what the Holy Spirit prompted Paul to write about in First Corinthians 13.

The emphasis of this lesson:

The Bible says that God's love does not demand its own way; it doesn't manipulate or scheme to get what it wants. His love is also not easily provoked, which means we don't act or speak in a needling way to cause an ugly response in others. Likewise, when God's love is working in us, we don't keep a record of the wrongs we have suffered — we forgive.

First Corinthians 13:4-8: The Love Test

In the previous three lessons, we have been examining what we are calling *The Love Test*, which is found in First Corinthians 13. Like a mirror, these verses help us see how well we are reflecting the love of God in our lives. And they bring attention to where we are falling short of His standards and need to self-correct. The apostle Paul opens the chapter by telling us how others perceive us when we don't walk in love. He said, "Though I speak with the tongues of men and of angels, and have not charity [love], I am become as sounding brass, or a tinkling cymbal" (1 Corinthians 13:1).

Taking into account the original Greek meaning of the words in this verse, here is the *Renner Interpretive Version (RIV)* of First Corinthians 13:1:

Even if I converse fluently in the languages of men and of angels, but do not possess love, then it's all nothing more than empty, hollow sounds. People like this, who claim to be super-spiritual but lack love, sound a lot like the nonstop banging and clanging of pagan brass instruments in your city that you wish would stop. Those who go around pretending to be deeply spiritual, but who are sorely deficient in love, are so annoying that when you feel trapped in a vicinity near them, you'll begin to look for any way to escape from being trapped with them. Even if they may say all the right things, their lack of love makes them as grating on your nerves as the clanging brass instruments that make you want to scream, 'Stop it and stop it now!' Let's be honest — these super-spiritual motor-mouths talk incessantly about how spiritual they are, but their absence of love makes it nothing more than a bunch of verbal hullabaloo. The hyped-up spiritual talk of these folks who demonstrate zero love to match their words is so offensive and nauseating that it can nearly call your flesh to battle just to get them to shut up.

For a detailed overview of the meaning of the phrases "sounding brass" and "tinkling cymbal," please refer back to Lesson 1 for a review.

Paul went on to describe how the *agape* love of God acts and doesn't act in First Corinthians 13:4-8:

Charity [love] suffereth long, and is kind; charity [love] envieth not; charity [love] vaunteth not itself, is not puffed up, doth not behave itself unseemly, seeketh not her own, is not easily provoked, thinketh no evil; rejoiceth not in iniquity, but rejoiceth in the truth; beareth all things, believeth all things, hopeth all things, endureth all things. Charity [love] never faileth....

The word "charity" in these verses is the Greek word *agape*, which describes the purest kind of love there is — the God-kind of love. To refresh your understanding of the deep meaning of this word, as well as the meaning of the words "suffereth long" and "kind," please refer back to Lesson 2. For a review of First Corinthians 13:4 and the beginning of verse 5, where Paul talks about how love does *not* behave, please refer back to Lesson 3.

Love 'Seeketh Not Her Own'

The apostle Paul continues his description of God's *agape* love saying, "[Love] doth not behave itself unseemly, seeketh not her own, is not easily provoked, thinketh no evil" (1 Corinthians 13:5). Notice the word "seeketh." It is a translation of the Greek word *zeteo*, and in a negative sense, it depicts *one so upset about not getting what he wants that he turns to the court system to sue or to demand what he wants to obtain.* This is *a person so intent on getting his own way that he will search, seek, and investigate, never giving up in his pursuit to get what he wants.* The word *zeteo* could also denote *a scheming individual who manipulates people, events, or circumstances until he finally gets what he wants.*

So when the Bible says love "…seeketh not her own…" (1 Corinthians 13:5), it means that when God's agape love is operating in us, we do not manipulate others. We don't use and abuse the court system, nor do we twist the facts, look for loopholes, or put words in other people's mouths to get our own way. When we are walking in love, we have no hidden schemes or agendas.

Taking into account the original Greek meaning of this word, here is the *Renner Interpretive Version (RIV)* of this part of First Corinthians 13:5:

> **Love does not manipulate situations, or scheme and devise methods that will twist situations to its own advantage.**

Love Is 'Not Easily Provoked'

In his next breath, Paul added, "…[Love] is not easily provoked…" (1 Corinthians 13:5). What's interesting about this part of the verse is that in the original Greek text, the word "easily" does not appear. The Greek simply says, "Love is not provoked." The word "easily" was inserted by the King James translators, and historians say it may have been added to send a subliminal message to King James, who happened to be the reigning king at that time. Apparently, he was a man who *easily* lost his temper and flew into a rage. So to encourage him to remain in control, the translators added the word "easily" into the text.

When the Bible says that love is not "provoked," it uses the Greek word *paroxsuno*, which is a compound of the words *para* and *oxsus*. The word *para* means *alongside*, and the word *oxsus* means *to poke, to prick, or to stick, as with a sharpened instrument*. When these two words are compounded to form the word *paroxsuno*, it portrays *someone who comes alongside another and then begins to poke, prick, or stick that other person with some type of sharpened instrument in order to enrage them*. He continues to pick, poke, and stick until the victim becomes provoked. The word *paroxsuno* can also mean *to call into combat; to irritate, to incite, to anger, to inflame, or to enrage; to provoke*.

Interestingly, Luke used this same word in Acts 15:39 when he described the major disagreement that erupted between the apostle Paul and Barnabas. As the two were making plans to head out on their second missionary journey, Barnabas wanted to take along his nephew John Mark. But because John Mark had deserted them on their first journey, Paul didn't want to take him again.

The Bible says, "And the contention was so sharp between them, that they departed asunder one from the other…" (Acts 15:39). The word "contention" here is the Greek word *paroxsuno*, the same word translated as "provoked" in First Corinthians 13:5. This tells us that Paul and Barnabas came right alongside of each other (*para*) and began to (*oxsus*) poke, prick, and provoke each other. Their behavior was ungodly and certainly not what should be demonstrated by men of God.

The truth is, anyone can begin acting in fleshly ways, and that is what happened to Paul and Barnabas. In fact, the second part of the word *paroxsuno* — the word *oxsus* — is the same Greek word for *vinegar*, which tells us that the words Paul and Barnabas exchanged during their heated argument were *sour, tart, bitter*, and *severe*. The needling between them became so intense that it broke their fellowship. The tight-knit friendship they had shared since Barnabas went and found Paul in Tarsus and brought him to the church at Antioch to do ministry together was severed — all because they gave in to their old nature and began acting in the flesh, provoking one another in the wrong way.

It is possible that when Paul wrote "…[Love] is not easily provoked…" in First Corinthians 13:5, he was regretfully remembering the moment when he acted unlovingly toward Barnabas, and the two went their separate ways.

Taking into account the original Greek meaning of this word, here is the *Renner Interpretive Version (RIV)* of this part of First Corinthians 13:5:

Love does not deliberately engage in actions or speak words that are so sharp, they cause an ugly or violent response.

Love 'Thinketh No Evil'

In addition to love not being easily provoked, Paul said, "...[Love] thinketh no evil" (1 Corinthians 13:5). The word "thinketh" in this verse is the Greek word *logidzomai*, which means *to mathematically count, calculate, or tabulate or to make a conclusion.* This word was used in the bookkeeping world to portray *the idea of a balance sheet or a profit-and-loss statement that a bookkeeper prepared at the end of the month or year.* Furthermore, the word *logidzomai* means *to make a calculation* or *to keep meticulous records.*

In this verse, Paul was not referring to a financial bookkeeper, but rather an offended believer who keeps detailed records of every wrong that has ever been done to him. Whenever someone mistreats him — or he perceives he has been mistreated — he makes a record of the infraction in his mental ledger. Every disappointment, every injustice, every grievance, every mistake that anyone has committed against this person has been recorded and tallied for future reference.

Friend, this is not the way the real love of God behaves. Think about it. How did God act when mankind sinned against Him? The Bible says, "For God so loved the world, that he gave his only begotten Son, that whosoever believeth in him should not perish, but have everlasting life" (John 3:16). Scripture also says, "If we confess our sins, he is faithful and just to forgive us our sins, and to cleanse us from all unrighteousness" (1 John 1:9). We are promised, "As far as the east is from the west, so far hath he removed our transgressions from us" (Psalm 103:12).

Now, this doesn't mean that God loses His memory, because He is all-knowing. It simply means that He has chosen to permanently put the record of our sins out of His mind. Once our past sins are nailed to the Cross with Christ and under His Blood, those evil actions are separated from us forever! That's how the *agape* love of God behaves. It forgives!

Taking into account the original Greek meaning of this word, here is the *Renner Interpretive Version (RIV)* of this part of First Corinthians 13:5:

Love does not deliberately keep records of wrongs or past mistakes.

When we take into account the original Greek meaning of each of the words we studied in this lesson, here is the *Renner Interpretive Version (RIV)* of First Corinthians 13:5:

> **Love doesn't manipulate situations, or scheme and devise methods that will twist situations to its own advantage; love does not deliberately engage in actions or speak words that are so sharp, they cause an ugly or violent response; love doesn't deliberately keep records of wrongs or past mistakes.**

What Does This Mean to You?

Friend, if there's anyone you're holding hostage in your mind because of something that they did to you, you need to release them and choose to forgive them. If you've never talked to them about how they treated you, that may be something you need to do. But once you've honestly confronted them and they have asked for forgiveness — or even if they haven't asked for forgiveness — you need to make a decision to move into the *agape* love of God and forgive them.

The fact is, if you continue to hold someone as a prisoner in your mind, your unwillingness to forgive them places you in a prison as well. The more you rehearse and nurse the wrong that they did to you, the more bitter you will become — and the stronger your prison will be. God doesn't want you to live incarcerated by unforgiveness another day. He wants you to release the one who hurt you and to let go of their offense.

"How can I do that?" you ask. Through the power of God's *agape* love that was shed abroad in your heart by the Holy Spirit the moment you were saved (*see* Romans 5:5). His supernatural love was liberally poured into your heart, and it is just waiting to move into action. All you need to do is release it, and the process begins by you humbling yourself and making the decision to forgive. It's time to throw away the record book you've been keeping of all the wrongs that have been done to you and begin to walk in the life-giving *agape* love of God!

STUDY QUESTIONS

Study to shew thyself approved unto God, a workman that needeth not to be ashamed, rightly dividing the word of truth.
— 2 Timothy 2:15

The Bible says, "For all have sinned, and come short of the glory of God" (Romans 3:23). Thankfully, it also says, "If we confess our sins, he [God] is faithful and just to forgive us our sins, and to cleanse us from all unrighteousness" (1 John 1:9).

1. What sobering statement about receiving God's forgiveness did Jesus make in Matthew 6:14 and 15? Had you ever seen or heard these words from Jesus before?

2. This truth is so vital that Jesus repeated it in a parable that is recorded in Matthew 18:23-35. Take a few moments to read this passage and share what new insights about forgiveness God is showing you.

3. According to Ephesians 4:32 and Colossians 3:13, what is one of the greatest reasons for you to forgive others?

4. Although Jesus' words in Luke 6:38 have often been quoted in connection with financial giving, they actually apply to forgiveness. Carefully read this passage, along with verse 37. What is the Holy Spirit speaking to you personally about how you forgive others?

PRACTICAL APPLICATION

But be ye doers of the word, and not hearers only, deceiving your own selves.
— James 1:22

1. According to First Corinthians 13:5, God's *love does not "seek its own,"* which means it does not demand its own way. How would you say you are doing in this area? Is there any situation you are in where you are so intent on getting your own way that you're searching, investigating, and relentlessly pursuing what you want? Are you scheming or manipulating people, events, or circumstances in an attempt to get your way? Have you become so upset about not getting what you want that you have even turned to the court system to file a suit? If so, how is this lesson helping you see your situation differently?

2. First Corinthians 13:5 also says that *love does not deliberately keep records of wrongs or past mistakes.* Be honest: Are you keeping a record of someone's wrongs — possibly someone you used to be close to? Who is it? What did they do to you that hurt you so deeply that you started keeping a running tab of their offenses?

3. The only way to experience true freedom and peace in your life is to choose to forgive those who have hurt you and release their offenses. Just as God has forgiven you of all the wrong things you have done, He desires and requires you to forgive others — and He gives you the power of His love to do it. If there is someone you know you need to forgive, pray this prayer:

Father, please forgive me for holding onto unforgiveness toward (insert person's name). *I release them into Your hands. You are the Judge, not me. You have forgiven me of so many things, and therefore, in obedience to Your Word, I choose to forgive* (insert person's name). *Please release Your love to heal my heart and flow through me to forgive* (insert person's name). *And as Your Word says in First Peter 3:9, I bless* (insert person's name) *with* (speak anything good that you would like to see happen in your own life). *Thank You, Father, for forgiving me and helping me to forgive and bless others. In Jesus name. Amen.*

TOPIC
Love Never Fails

SCRIPTURES

1. **1 Corinthians 13:1** — Though I speak with the tongues of men and of angels, and have not charity, I am become as sounding brass, or a tinkling cymbal.

2. **1 Corinthians 13:4-8** — Charity suffereth long, and is kind; charity envieth not; charity vaunteth not itself, is not puffed up, doth not behave itself unseemly, seeketh not her own, is not easily provoked, thinketh no evil; rejoiceth not in iniquity, but rejoiceth in the truth; beareth all things, believeth all things, hopeth all things, endureth all things. Charity never faileth....

GREEK WORDS

1. "rejoiceth not" — **οὐ χαίρει** (*ou chairei*): the word **οὐ** (*ou*) means no or not, and the word **χαίρει** (*chairei*) is from the word *chairo*, which is the Greek word for joy and carries the idea of being glad about something; it pictures a person who is euphoric over something that has happened; one who is overjoyed, elated, ecstatic, exhilarated, thrilled, jubilant, or even rapturous

2. "iniquity" — **ἀδικία** (*adikia*): injustice or something that is wrong or bad

3. "beareth" — **στέγω** (*stego*): to cover, as a roof covers a house; within the word is the concept of protection, exactly as a roof protects, shields, and guards the inhabitants of a house from exposure to the outside influences of weather; it describes shielding or guarding others from exposure; to guard the inhabitants of a house from exposure to the outside influences of weather; the roof is designed to shield people from storms, hurricanes, tornadoes, rain, hail, snow, wind, blistering hot temperatures, and so on; such protection is vital for survival in most climates and prevents people from freezing to death or burning as a result of continual exposure to sunlight

4. "believeth" — πιστεύω (*pisteuo*): to put one's faith or trust in something or someone; tense depicts a constant, continuous entrusting of one's faith in something or someone; involving a "never-give-up" kind of belief that something will turn out the very best; the phrase could actually be taken to mean that love "believes the best in every situation"

5. "hopeth" — ἐλπίζω (*elpidzo*): pictures one who places his hope in something and then keeps his hope there; carries the idea of an unwavering trust; not only a hope, but an expectation of good things

6. "endureth" — ὑπομονή (*hupomene*): to remain in one's spot; to keep a position; to resolve to maintain territory gained; to defiantly stick it out regardless of pressures mounted against it; staying power; hang-in-there power; the attitude that holds out, holds on, outlasts, perseveres, and hangs in there, never giving up, refusing to surrender to obstacles, and turning down every opportunity to quit; it pictures one who is under a heavy load but refuses to bend, break, or surrender

7. "never" — οὐδέποτε (*oudepote*): never ever, not at any time

8. "faileth" — πίπτω (*pipto*): to fall or collapse; a downward plummet; to fall from a high position; depicts falling into ruin, into destruction, into some kind of misfortune, or into disappointment; here, something that disappoints or fails

SYNOPSIS

Can you remember your wedding ceremony? For most couples, it is a joyous day of celebration. Over the years, many newlyweds in Moscow, Russia, have journeyed to what is called the Bridge of Love on their wedding day to publically declare their lifelong commitment to one another. Symbolically, they attach a personalized lock to one of the seven "love trees" that line the bridge. It's their way of saying to each other and the world, "We're locked in love to each other for the rest of our lives."

As sincere as these husbands and wives were on their wedding day, they were quickly met with the realization of how challenging it can be to actually walk in love. Good intentions and will power can only take us so far. The only way we can successfully walk in love is to crucify our flesh and allow the Holy Spirit to release the power of God's *agape* love in and through our lives.

The emphasis of this lesson:

When God's *agape* love is actively at work in our lives, we don't celebrate people's misfortunes; we rejoice when they're blessed. We guard and protect people from being exposed and believe the very best of them in every situation. God's love always hopes for and anticipates the best, endures and never quits, and it can be relied on in every situation.

In First Corinthians 13, the apostle Paul gives us what we call *The Love Test*, explaining how love acts and does not act. The purpose of this passage is not to make us feel condemned or guilty. It is meant to be a mirror to help us see how well we are reflecting the *agape* love of God and where we need His grace to self-correct and come up higher in our love walk. Under the anointing of the Holy Spirit, Paul wrote:

> Though I speak with the tongues of men and of angels, and have not charity [love], I am become as sounding brass, or a tinkling cymbal.
>
> [Love] charity suffereth long, and is kind; [love] charity envieth not; [love] charity vaunteth not itself, is not puffed up,
>
> [Love] doth not behave itself unseemly, seeketh not her own, is not easily provoked, thinketh no evil;
>
> [Love] rejoiceth not in iniquity, but rejoiceth in the truth;
>
> [Love] beareth all things, believeth all things, hopeth all things, endureth all things.
>
> [Love] Charity never faileth....
>
> 1 Corinthians 13:1,4-8

Remember, the word "charity" in these verses is the Greek word *agape*, which describes the purest kind of love there is — the supernatural, God-kind of love. To refresh your understanding of the deep meaning of the word *agape*, as well as the meaning of the words "suffereth long" and "kind," please refer back to Lesson 2.

We have seen that in First Corinthians 13:1, Paul tells us how we appear to others when we don't walk in love. He said, "Though I speak with the tongues of men and of angels, and have not charity [love], I am become as sounding brass, or a tinkling cymbal."

Taking into account the original Greek meaning of the words in this verse, here is the *Renner Interpretive Version (RIV)* of First Corinthians 13:1:

Even if I converse fluently in the languages of men and of angels, but do not possess love, then it's all nothing more than empty, hollow sounds. People like this, who claim to be super-spiritual but lack love, sound a lot like the nonstop banging and clanging of pagan brass instruments in your city that you wish would stop. Those who go around pretending to be deeply spiritual, but who are sorely deficient in love, are so annoying that when you feel trapped in a vicinity near them, you'll begin to look for any way to escape from being trapped with them. Even if they may say all the right things, their lack of love makes them as grating on your nerves as the clanging brass instruments that make you want to scream, 'Stop it and stop it now!' Let's be honest — these super-spiritual motor-mouths talk incessantly about how spiritual they are, but their absence of love makes it nothing more than a bunch of verbal hullabaloo. The hyped-up spiritual talk of these folks who demonstrate zero love to match their words is so offensive and nauseating that it can nearly call your flesh to battle just to get them to shut up.

For the background on this passage and the meaning of the phrases "sounding brass" and "a tinkling cymbal," please refer back to Lesson 1 for a review. And for a detailed overview of verses 4 and 5 of First Corinthians 13, where Paul talks about how love does *not* behave, please refer back to Lessons 3 and 4.

Love Does Not Celebrate the Misfortunes of Others

When we come to First Corinthians 13:6, Paul goes on to say, "[Love] rejoiceth not in iniquity, but rejoiceth in the truth." In Greek, the phrase "rejoiceth not" is *ou chairei*. The word *chairei* is from the word *chairo*, which is the Greek word for *joy* and carries the idea of *being glad about something*. It pictures *a person who is euphoric over something that has happened; one who is overjoyed, elated, ecstatic, exhilarated, thrilled, jubilant, or even rapturous*.

The word *ou*, which precedes *chairei* (rejoiceth), means *no* or *not*, and therefore negates or cancels out the rejoicing. This brings us to the word "iniquity," which is the Greek word *adikia*, and it describes *injustice* or *something that is wrong or bad*.

Taking into account the original Greek meaning of these words, here is the *Renner Interpretive Version (RIV)* of the first part of First Corinthians 13:6:

> **Love does not feel overjoyed when it sees an injustice done to someone else.**

This tells us that the *agape*, high-level love of God does not celebrate or become ecstatic and overjoyed when someone else experiences a misfortune — even if the person is reaping the harvest of their own bad seed they've planted. Instead, "…[Love] rejoiceth in the truth" (1 Corinthians 13:6).

Taking into account the same original Greek meaning of these words, here is the *Renner Interpretive Version (RIV)* of the second part of First Corinthians 13:6:

> **Love is elated, thrilled, ecstatic, and overjoyed with the truth.**

How you react when other people experience misfortunes or when someone is greatly blessed reveals your true level of spiritual maturity. When you look into the "mirror" of this particular verse, what do you see? Are you reflecting the *agape* love of God or the fleshly, conditional love of earth?

Love 'Beareth All Things'

In First Corinthians 13:7, Paul continues to expand our understanding of God's *agape* love, stating that "[Love] beareth all things…." The word "beareth" in this verse is the Greek word *stego*, which means *to cover, as a roof covers a house*. What is interesting is that within this word is the concept of *protection*, exactly as a roof protects, shields, and guards the inhabitants of a house from exposure to the outside influences of weather.

Thus, the word *stego* — translated here as "beareth" — means *to guard the inhabitants of a house from exposure to the outside influences of weather*. Just as the roof is designed to shield people from storms, hurricanes, tornadoes, rain, hail, snow, wind, blistering hot temperatures, and so on, God's *agape* love acts in the same way. Such protection is vital for survival in most climates and prevents people from freezing to death or burning as a result of continual exposure to sunlight.

The fact that the Holy Spirit prompted Paul to use this word *stego* to describe love tells us that there are many unpredictable seasons in life. Although there are times of sunny and pleasant conditions, there are also stormy seasons, frigid seasons, and seasons of intense heat. When we are exposed to and assaulted by difficult external circumstances, God's real love in us "beareth" — *stego* — all things. This means, instead of exposing people's faults and weaknesses when they are being pelted by problems, we cover and protect them. Aren't you thankful that God has blessed you with people who have shielded and guarded you?

Taking into account the original Greek meaning of this word, here is the *Renner Interpretive Version (RIV)* of this part of First Corinthians 13:7:

> **Love protects, shields, guards, covers, conceals, and safeguards people from exposure.**

Love 'Believeth All Things'

Not only does love bear all things, it also "…believeth all things…" (1 Corinthians 13:7). The word "believeth" here is the Greek word *pisteuo*, which means *to put one's faith or trust in something or someone*. The tense depicts *a constant, continuous entrusting of one's faith in something or someone — involving a "never-give-up" kind of belief that something will turn out the very best*. The phrase "believeth all things" could actually be taken to mean that love "believes the best in every situation."

Of course, this does not mean that love is blind to things that are bad and ugly — or that it ignores problems. What it means is that God's *agape* love is so filled with faith that it pushes through disturbing issues it sees and chooses to believe the best about that individual or group of people. Rather than pick their faults to pieces, love strains forward and expects to see the highest potential that abides in every person.

One of the best examples of this kind of love in action is in the relationship between a parent and their children. Oftentimes our kids will behave or perform below our expectations. It is in those moments we must ask the Holy Spirit to release God's *agape* love in us toward our children. With His help, we can choose to believe the best about them — that the Word, which has been planted in their hearts, and the Spirit who is involved in their lives, will work in them to turn things around for the better.

Taking into account the original Greek meaning of this word, here is the *Renner Interpretive Version (RIV)* of this part of First Corinthians 13:7:

Love strains forward with all its might to believe the very best in every situation.

Love 'Hopeth All Things'

In addition to bearing all things and believing all things, Paul said, "… [Love] hopeth all things…" (1 Corinthians 13:7). The word "hopeth" here is a translation of the Greek word *elpidzo*, which pictures *one who places his hope in something or someone and then keeps his hope there*. This word carries *the idea of an unwavering trust*; it is not only a hope, but *an expectation of good things*.

When someone has disappointed us and failed to meet our expectations again and again, our natural tendency is to assume they will fail again or perform poorly just as they have in the past. But God's supernatural love in us responds in just the opposite way. Instead of expecting another bad performance, love has a fixed expectation that this person is going to begin to improve and perform differently — that in spite of their past, they are going to do well in life.

Taking into account the original Greek meaning of this word, here is the *Renner Interpretive Version (RIV)* of this part of First Corinthians 13:7:

Love always expects and anticipates the best in others and the best for others.

Love 'Endureth All Things'

The last aspect of love that the apostle Paul mentions in First Corinthians 13:7 is "…[Love] endureth all things." In Greek, the word "endureth" is a translation of the word *hupomene*, which means *to remain in one's spot; to keep a position; to resolve to maintain territory gained*. It can also mean *to defiantly stick it out regardless of pressures mounted against it*. The word *hupomene* describes *staying power* or *hang-in-there power*. It is *the attitude that holds out, holds on, outlasts, perseveres, and hangs in there, never giving up, refusing to surrender to obstacles, and turning down every opportunity to quit.* Furthermore, it pictures *one who is under a heavy load but refuses to bend, break, or surrender.*

The use of the word *hupomene* tells us that God's love says, "I'm committed to you. Regardless of what things look like, how much it costs, or the odds that are against us, I'm staying with you until we see a breakthrough and victory is achieved."

Taking into account the original Greek meaning of this word, here is the *Renner Interpretive Version (RIV)* of this part of First Corinthians 13:7:

Love never quits, never surrenders, and never gives up.

When we insert the original Greek meaning of each of these words, here is the *Renner Interpretive Version (RIV)* of First Corinthians 13:7:

Love protects, shields, guards, covers, conceals, and safeguards people from exposure; love strains forward with all its might to believe the very best in every situation; love always expects and anticipates the best in others and the best for others; love never quits, never surrenders, and never gives up.

Love 'Never Faileth'

Paul concluded his description of love in First Corinthians 13:8 by declaring, "[Love] never faileth...." The word "faileth" in this verse is a form of the Greek word *pipto*, which means *to fall or collapse.* It can also indicate *a downward plummet* or *to fall from a high position.* This word has been used to depict *falling into ruin, into destruction, into some kind of misfortune, or into disappointment.* Here, it signifies *something that disappoints or fails.*

Paul said, "[Love] never faileth..." (1 Corinthians 13:8). The word "never" in Greek means *never ever, not at any time.* Hence, God's supernatural, *agape* love will never ever disappoint you or let you down at any time. Even when people you greatly respect and admire let you down, you can always, and at all times and in every situation, rely and depend on the love of God.

Keep in mind all of us have moments when we're disappointed in someone. Likewise, there have been moments when we, too, have been a disappointment to others. So if someone has let you down and not lived up to your expectations, don't be judgmental or hold a grudge. Instead, pray for them and believe the best for them. Remember, someone forgave you and was patient with you and stayed with you. Let God's love flow through you to offer the same strength to someone else.

Taking into account the original Greek meaning of the words we have studied in these five lessons, here is the *Renner Interpretive Version (RIV)* of First Corinthians 13:4-8:

> Love patiently and passionately bears with others for as long as patience is needed and does not easily give up or bow out; love doesn't demand others to be like itself; rather, it is so focused on the needs of others that it bends over backwards to become what others need it to be; love is not ambitious, self-centered, or so consumed with itself that it never thinks of the needs or desires of others; love doesn't go around talking about itself all the time, constantly exaggerating and embellishing the facts to make it look more important in the sight of others; love does not behave in a prideful, arrogant, haughty, superior, snooty, snobbish, or clannish manner; love is not rude and discourteous — it is not careless or thoughtless, nor does it carry on in a fashion that is insensitive to others; love does not manipulate situations, or scheme and devise methods that will twist situations to its own advantage; love does not deliberately provoke others by engaging in actions or speaking words that are so sharp, they cause an ugly response; love does not deliberately keep records of wrongs or past mistakes; love does not feel overjoyed when it sees an injustice done to someone else, but is elated, thrilled, ecstatic, and overjoyed with the truth; love protects, shields, guards, covers, conceals, and safeguards people from exposure; love strains forward with all its might to believe the very best in every situation; love always expects and anticipates the best in others and for others; love never quits, never surrenders, and never gives up; love never disappoints, never fails, and never ever lets anyone down.

Remember, the purpose of these verses in First Corinthians 13 is not to make you feel condemned or guilty. They are meant to be a mirror to help you see how well you are reflecting the *agape* love of God. As you work through the study and application questions, listen for the voice of the Holy Spirit to see where you need His grace to self-correct and come up higher in your love walk.

STUDY QUESTIONS

> Study to shew thyself approved unto God, a workman that needeth
> not to be ashamed, rightly dividing the word of truth.
> — 2 Timothy 2:15

1. As we come to this final lesson of *The Love Test*, what would you say is your greatest takeaway from this study? What do you most want to remember about God's *agape* love — and share with others?

2. Of all the different life-giving aspects of God's love toward you, what characteristic do you most appreciate and value? Why is this one so special to you?

3. The essence of walking in love is being *others-focused*, not self-focused. Carefully read Luke 9:23,24; Galatians 2:20; Romans 12:1; and First Corinthians 15:31, and identify the key to being others-focused.

PRACTICAL APPLICATION

> But be ye doers of the word, and not hearers only,
> deceiving your own selves.
> — James 1:22

1. Be honest. Have you ever secretly rejoiced when something bad happened to someone whose actions were known to be evil? Did you think to yourself, *Well it's about time. They're finally getting a dose of what they've been dishing out — the law of sowing and reaping is finally kicking in?* Knowing that true love doesn't rejoice over the misfortune of others, how is the Holy Spirit redirecting your response to such situations? (*Consider* Proverbs 24:17; Matthew 5:44; Romans 12:20.)

2. Likewise, are you able to celebrate when other people are blessed? When something good happens in someone else's life, do you become jealous or joyful? (*Consider* Romans 12:15.)

3. When we're exposed to and assaulted by difficult external circumstances, God's love covers and protects us. Who has God brought into *your* life to shield you, instead of exposing your faults and weaknesses? What do you most appreciate about their friendship? Who is presently going through a stormy season that God is asking you to guard and protect? (*Consider* First Peter 4:8; Proverbs 17:9.)

4. The Bible tells us that God's love in us *strains forward with all its might to believe the very best in every situation.* How are you doing with

regards to this facet of love? Is there someone at home, at work, or at church you are struggling to believe the best about? Who is it? Take time to pray and ask the Holy Spirit to remind you of the times He has placed people in your life who believed the best about you when you were at your worst. Then ask Him for strength to believe the best about this person. (*Consider* Galatians 6:1,2; Romans 15:1,2; Matthew 7:1-5.)

Notes

.